COLLECTED WORKS

Frans (François Henricus Anthonia) van Dixhoorn was born in 1948 in Hansweert, Zeeland, in the south of the Netherlands. Shortly after the North Sea flood of 1953, the family moved to Vlissingen. In 1972, he became a teacher at the primary school in Nieuw- en St. Joosland, just outside Middelburg. He remained at this school for seventeen years, and taught oral and written language expression at various schools in the area. In 1986, he moved to Amsterdam, where he lived for ten years before returning to Middelburg. He became a full-time artist from the mid-1980s: at first mainly with visual work (although this did not lead to exhibitions) and from the early 1990s as a poet. Van Dixhoorn has published seven collections, all with De Bezige Bij. He is the recipient of the C. Buddingh Prize for best first collection (1994), the Woordlijst Prize (2007) and he is a 2012 Ida Gerhard Prize and VSB-Prize nominee. In 2009, the translation of the first three collections was published in French by Le bleu du ciel; and his work has been translated into German, where it has been set to music and toured nationally.

Astrid Alben is a poet, editor and translator. Her translation of Anne Vegter's *Island glacier mountain* won an English PEN Translates Award in 2022. She is the international commissioning editor at Prototype Publishing.

Also by Astrid Alben

Little Dead Rabbit	(Prototype, 2022)
Island, mountain, glacier (translated)	(Prototype, 2022)
Klein dood konijn	(PoëzieCentrum, 2021)
Plainspeak	(Prototype, 2019)
Ai! Ai! Pianissimo	(Arc Publications, 2011)

Also by F. van Dixhoorn

Verre uittrap	(De Bezige Bij, 2017)
De zon in de pan	(De Bezige Bij, 2012)
Twee piepjes	(De Bezige Bij, 2007)
Dan op de zeevaartschool	(De Bezige Bij, 2003)
Takken molenwater / Kastanje jo / Hakke tonen /	
Uiterton / Molen in de zon	(De Bezige Bij, 2000)
Armzwaai / Grote keg / Loodswezen I	(De Bezige Bij, 1997)
Jaagpad / Rust in de tent / Zwaluwen vooruit	(De Bezige Bij , 1994)

Collected Works

F. van Dixhoorn
Translated by Astrid Alben

Broken Sleep Books

**N ederlands letterenfonds
dutch foundation
for literature**

Published with the support of the
Dutch Foundation for Literature

© 2023 Astrid Alben. All rights reserved; no part of this book may be reproduced by any means without the publisher's permission.

ISBN: 978-1-915760-90-6

The author has asserted their right to be identified as the author of this Work in accordance with the Copyright, Designs and Patents Act 1988

Cover designed by Aaron Kent

Typeset by Aaron Kent

Broken Sleep Books Ltd	Broken Sleep Books Ltd
Rhydwen	Fair View
Talgarreg	St Georges Road
Ceredigion	Cornwall
SA44 4HB	PL26 7YH

CONTENTS

Translator's Note	7
Towpath (1994)	13
All quiet (1994)	35
Swallows go (1994)	67
Arm signal (1997)	101
Big batten (1997)	127
Pilotage I (1997)	139
Muddled molenwater (2000)	161
Chestnut joe (2000)	171
Hack tones (2000)	181
Hack tones (2000)	191
Outer buoy (2000)	201
Mill in the sun (2000)	211
All at sea (2003)	221
Two peeps (2007)	251
The sun in the pan (2012)	283
4. The sun in the pan (2012)	301
Drop kick (2017)	319
Acknowledgments	369

TRANSLATOR'S NOTE

F. van Dixhoorn's work has garnered major literary prizes since his debut poetry collection *Towpath / All quiet / Swallows go* in 1994, while remaining controversial and divisive. This *Collected Works* marks the first time that Van Dixhoorn's poems will reach an English readership. To new readers coming into contact with the work, my advice is to keep in mind the following four factors that are crucial to Van Dixhoorn's methodology and aesthetics:

1. There is in the poems an **equality** between past, present and future. Equality of metre, rhythm, cadence. There is equality in what gets attention and what is relevant. There is equality between the words 'minuscule', 'the', 'overpass', 'turn' and 'air bubbles' are all equal. This equality is what operates the poems and what is manifest in their construction. And all things being equal, construction is also *mis*construction. There is equality between private language -our interior monologue- and language that connects us to others and the exterior world. The absence of punctuation that would suggest a narrative or at the minimum an interrelatedness between the lines keeps you second-guessing and tuned in, as it were, to a radio station with a faltering signal. The world can't be put in order and poetry is ideally placed to reflect that.

2. The poem as **landscape** is crucial to Van Dixhoorn: the size of the margins, the choice of font, the colour on the cover, the dimensions of the page, the placement of the stanza on the page, which, including any blank lines, each count sixteen lines, so that when you close his books and stack them, the poems form a block with six sides. The poet's commitment to straight lines. The landscape of the poem informs the form: all is at work to make the poem work.

Van Dixhoorn's choice of subjects is classical - referencing spring, nature, the elements, overpasses and bridges:

> 1. for the water level / dark and still / lasts now / as long as I
> want / this year / spring has come / early

[Pilotage I]

Nonetheless, the distinctive qualities of these poems stem not from its subject matter but from the poet's methodology: Van Dixhoorn's poems are not so much *about* landscape, not even as a metaphor for human experience: landscape dictates the form.

3. Barbara Hepworth famously stated that all her early memories were of forms and shapes and textures. "Moving through and over the West Riding landscape with my father in his car, the hills were sculptures; the roads defined the form." How we look at things, from what angle we observe, and whether that be with the eye or in the mind, perspective dominates the work.

There's a paradox at the core of Van Dixhoorn's oeuvre, which is to do with **perspective**. Read the poem at a detached distance and the by and large random observations, snippets of conversations, idioms and exclamations stacked on top of one another make sense. The poems seem perfectly accessible. Yet when you read the poems more closely they seem to fall apart. Instead of things becoming clearer, as I read and reread the poems, the more I familiarised myself with the work and gained in understanding and perspective, the more intimate my relationship grew with the text — the more incoherent and confusing the poems. Syntax shifts like quicksand, reshaping and remoulding both the text and the act of reading. For me as the translator, this was exciting and exasperating in equal measure.

4. The poems manage their symptomatic lack of continuity without letting the whole drift into something hollow or disjointed. This baffled me. How can a poem so confidently not be about something? How does it communicate? How do I translate the

work? Van Dixhoorn's poems started me thinking about what poetry is. Finally, it is important to understand that every poem is part of the **aesthetic whole**. Without metaphor or simile within the poems, the poems *themselves* become a metaphor for how we look at the world outside of the poems and for the act of reading. All the usual ways of discussing a poem are rendered nugatory: there is no story or plot, no theme, there are no characters or emotions to analyse. Van Dixhoorn looks beyond the single poem to the artistic project ahead.

***

One summer, many years ago, Van Dixhoorn and I cycled together from his home in Middelburg to Domburg, a seaside town tucked into the dunes along a part of the North Sea coast. Van Dixhoorn and I seldom discuss his work. Typically, he bats away my queries. We peddled on through the landscape of his birth and most of his life, this man-made landscape of sluices, dikes, cranes, basalt blocks, storm barriers and the bobbing waterline of a cargo ship. Pumping stations continually drained excess water from these wet zones that nestled down peacefully like a dozing child, and the glaucous, lead-green water of the delta turned outwards where we saw offshore wind turbines, groynes wading into sea, storm surge barriers and bridges connecting industrial complexes under constant stress and construction.

We cycled through this landscape of lines and grids and observed how land consolidates land, how it is systematised to a highest degree: potato fields, a shelter belt, urbanisation, the infrastructures of roads, docklands and watercourses.

I remarked how the poplars appeared to snap to attention as we cycled past and I craned my neck to see the container ships towering two metres above us with humps of sand and gravel like a caravan of elephants moving through the dunes, and shared with him that it was as if this landscape, at two metres below sea-level, of construction and reconstruction could be taken as a blueprint for the designed functionality of his own poems, that it was as if we were cycling through his poems; and it came as a surprise, a sweet gift, when he confided to me that as a child, then as student at teacher training college, later as a local schoolmaster, and even to this day Van Dixhoorn counts the trees on his daily cycle route along the towpaths: 1. 2. 3. 4. 1. 2. 3.

***

How do you translate *that*?

***

I don't want the words to be, I need the words to *do*.

***

Little breakthroughs and triumphs in the translation were swept away by the next line —

***

What if the poems (and even individual lines) are miniature sketches without beginning or end, not unlike Morton Feldman's repetitive minimal music, which he often listens to whilst working?

***

Takken molenwater is the title of this poem from his third collection. The literal translation of 'molenwater' is 'mill water'. However, 'molenwater' is also the name of the street on which Van Dixhoorn lives.

***

I was introduced to Van Dixhoorn's poems by a poet with whom I sat on the editorial board of a literary journal. The journal was short-lived but our friendship stuck. Young, ambitious and as yet unpublished, we critiqued each other's early work and were competitive enough to be of use to each other for a time. New to Amsterdam from London, I had asked her to introduce me to contemporary Dutch poets. Not long after, she took me along to a poetry event at De Melkweg. That was in 2001. Van Dixhoorn already had a head full of wispy white hair sticking out and as he paced up and down through the space his head moved along with his body like a cloud. Clearly, he was in a hurry to kick off proceedings, to get the readings underway, as if he had somewhere else to be, or, as I learned later, if we weren't here for the poetry, why be here at all? His playful, determined impatience was infectious, for he is also curious, a trait I perceive as an expression of kindness. Not exactly shy, but introverted. He read from his work with the pitched focus yet easily distracted mien of a train conductor updating passengers on arrival and departure times.

After the reading, my friend ushered me into his life as "your future English translator." Initial pleasantries were quickly exchanged: "Van Dixhoorn. But friends call me Dix, and so does everyone else. Call me Dix."

— Astrid Alben
18 April 2023

TOWPATH

1. nevertheless it's clear
how quiet the woods are here
seen from the front
2. among the trees I come to four
always the same not
comparable
among the trees I come to four
always the same not
comparable
surely therefore from right
to left a coat
which you want to show
so go on show
3. starting point
4. they'll probably leave today
he's wearing the same

as when they came
1. the actress is right
they'll probably leave today
he's wearing the same
as when they came
2. on the one hand
I think you should go
on the other hand
you can't stay still either
when no one hears you
the grass
behind the green table
mousey men who fall in love
with young girls
unaware of their existence
3. nevertheless it's clear

how quiet the woods are here
seen from the front
4. through the middle of the field
a road
until someone had the idea
to look on the other side
after all there's woods there too
1. at the circumference of the tree
the father and mother lie near the tent
an extenuating circumstance
they fell asleep
2. rehearsal
always in the distance that lorry
the brass band isn't in uniform
there's no way they can meet
they're all going at the same speed

I often think
I would have liked to have been there
how old they would have been now
3. at the circumference of the tree
the father and mother lie near the tent
an extenuating circumstance
they fell asleep
4. splash
was about to dismount
to pick up the ball as well
let's see it's easier
to say nothing
keep it to oneself
1. towpath
which you need to cross
swans without a neck float

set the agenda
in the other hand an orange
which has been on the table all day
it has been pencilled on rolled and pricked
2. an orange
as a result
of the performance
the first gesture comes about
quite naturally
during the lunch break
geese fly overhead
3. two swans in a wider circle
he never looks
while the production is taking place
he can't talk
4. may I

sit in between
the two of you
there's no one
as precise as he
1. what's it called again
I'll take it
before I forget
actually it's not as simple as that
what gets in the way
I'd like to get home by eleven for once too
2. lack of space for a summary
in effect no difference in strength
when rereading
in effect flipping back to the beginning
so that later I can recognise them
as a performance

3. I'm not getting on the table
if that's what you think
whatever made you think that
falls silent
4. definitely use
and you can talk
you can read what it says
the duckling rolls out of the handkerchief
once on the same table
the little bird collapses
suddenly disappeared into thin air
some tiptoe around the box
1. slowly tip and pour
the first ones are starting
to get curious
but the bottom

stays black and motionless
his steel feathers
2. dook: what am I forgetting
finie: you let me go
3. and ask for a stamp
is it necessary
confusing one place for another
and while you're at it
you might as well check
to see what we'll be eating
4. by not thinking
the same over and over
the boat has
become incredibly bigger
when nothing is done
the collection risks

falling apart
this summer
1. or do we stay
connected
to each other
so that we
stick up for each other
2. what's in that box
you can't just stand there
who'll step up when you step down
shrugs her shoulders
what more of yourself
can you put in
3. more of a browsing than searching
both crop up once
moreover towards the sun

how to divide the available attention
bearing in mind the tourists
who in summer couldn't care less
about change
4. can go together
in succession when the sun shines
they have to stand outside
do you like it
just half
then you turn it over
and pay for half
do you like it
just half
then you turn it over
and pay for half
1. inside when

quiet is coming
starlings from the meadow
patricia
simply adores horses
you'll be seeing her
at the weekend
2. a removal van outside michiel de ruyter
the driver winds down the window
thousands are returning from the beach
the following will hold
if crucq comes for me I'm not in
3. one after the other
yes monday
just makes no sense
for a wide audience
you use fewer objects

for an overview than yesterday
4. let's wait for each other
or shall I carry the bag
you can't hear me anyway
this is no sea
the sun rises in the east
and sets in the sea
1. just toss them apart
and then just toss them outside
preferably with everyone there
their faces pressed together
2. follow me outside
crummy bike
to have one's portrait done
in another position
is a way not to meet

3. muddled water
the opposite of yellow
now be smart
a stroll from one side
to the other
has to be a part of
throwing
do I know what I'm doing
4. mid july
for half of it
I don't get changed
I don't change
at all
1. don't think it's because it's july
stands with a newspaper
wrapped around a fish

so good
2. first of all it's summer
and equidistant
except for folding the map
skipping the difference
you don't have to say anything
what you say makes sense
I always leave things slightly open
whatever it's in
3. in the final half
the appearance of the moon
reality bent out of shape
from one thing to another
music
4. overpass
probably this place was chosen too well

how else to explain that
people ignore the information provided
four children dangle their legs
the attention has lapsed
if they come any closer the animal will bolt
1. are you camping here
you gave me a fright
I heard someone come past
and couldn't see who it was
2. closing off the same side
we lost that lorry finally
the waves move in the same direction
keep persisting
marijke mixes up the rivers
intervalos azules
3. a road

cuts through the middle of the field
until someone had the idea
to look on the other side
after all there's woods there too
4. damaged only
it's yellow and invisible
if every gesture produces a sound
then every gesture
is preceded by a sound
1. illustrative sounds
2. what I like
the cool precision
that is evoked
to escape from that cloud
to the riverbank
to cut off the corner

not a twig breaks his fall
3. come autumn
it's purple and round the back
to surprise the audience
you have to surprise yourself
find a system
behind which to disappear
4. among the trees I come to four
still the same not
comparable
among the trees I come to four
still the same not
comparable
surely therefore from right
to left a coat
which you want to show

so go on show
1. why repeat
sunbathing on the slope
calms me down
I think because it's a report
if another one is needed
and relates to water
2. sighs
grows calmer
if another one is needed
3. sighs why all three
seems more calm
opposite each other and also
under the overpass
I know to find this brick
4. therein talk

on the bottom side by side
at the top against the same
moon
1. the moon
which slowly climbs
in her cold light
wild dogs glide by
stand still and take in the air
of the lonely monkey
2. draw a loop
through the air
must be a bridge
to be sure
they shout a bridge
3. for the rest it's quiet
going the distance

how quiet it is
which doesn't count
4. yet it is
not just
that silence this lack of incident
that is responsible for
1. mieke hold on fast
to the branches of the trees
mieke hold on fast
to the branches of the mast
2. a bend in the road
instead of coming yourself
clouds pass
3. whence through an orange megaphone
return
4. this evening let's try fish

ALL QUIET

1. by the way I must say
I was shocked
by the reaction to that ball
2. drop kick
3. before dinner

I will reach the sea
before dinner
I will reach the sea
 1. nonsense
waiting in the direction
for it to happen
I don't know
if there's more you can ask
simultaneously
2. let's wait for each other

or shall I carry that bag
you can't hear me anyway
this is no sea
the sun rises in the east
and sets in the sea

3. at the same time utterly new
going for a walk going for dinner
with the same intensity
we talk about fishing
sometimes about the west
1. further down it's quiet
life only starts
after the game
though dismissed as dissimilar
by the spectators

I miss the water
2. the grass is yellow
where they swam
they all burst out laughing
swimming

won't get you very far
other than back to the clothes
3. and again
how warm it is
being short of clothes
but then again no
complaining is part of survival
1. violent punch
2. the size of that boat
you'll never get the scent

out of those clothes
swimming
will never get you anywhere
other than back to the clothes
3. if I'm not mistaken

I have a knife
there you see
1. fancy looking out over sea
while I eat
where does listening end
when is it eavesdropping
the heart's pounding louder than
the conversation being eavesdropped
2. you the same again
but so different to the same

hanging by one arm from a beam
we grew accustomed to each other
some played music
nico played the monkey
3. pure bliss

1. the size of that fish
dressed for summer on the one hand
on the other there's that agreement distance
to talk to each other
about when it's
said and done
2. look the sea
in starving people
you can see their faces distort
or if listening to

another voice
is deadly tiring
3. oh well
for now there's work
hammering together

a bridge
1. a lot of luggage on both sides
clumsily stacked together
see what happens
whoever jumps up
will lift the entire box
into the air
2. a shoe
not asking
for myself

am I satisfied
is the fire
less important
than the work
3. who is nico

1. in addition to
interrupting the meal
what did I forget
jumped ahead
if there are no questions
at least let them
remain unanswered
2. his cap
 is against the sun
doesn't think to stop

sadly enough
I'll keep carrying on
until I'm satisfied
3. across a chair
1. then looking out

across the water
the grass and the hum
we sing what we know
when we remember
we give it
another name
2. to be sure
in the sand
never a moment's quiet
constantly busy

never a moment's quiet
who's brave enough
to scream let's eat
from the same place as me
3. full in the face

and it doesn't surprise me
however loud I shout
you're worn out
1. if those are being used
it can't be called patience
see that yellow circle over there
that's a sand line
in the middle
stands a large lorry
2. not tonight

the pipes are rusting
if they're still there
this coming winter
they'll burst
3. the grass is too long

to hurry things along
hold conversations
everyone starts at once
did they think we were the enemy
1. for each other
abroad
I think so
you hardly know what you're eating
keep your mind
on the food

2. enormous brake
3. among the leaves
gently swaying cages
the questions come up
the organisation used to be banned

all recognised each other
this homesickness shocks us
1. that's right on paper
even if it's only about
going when we go
the singing starts
even if it's ever so small
there has to be a threat
2. if I'm not mistaken
I have a knife

there you see
no one is satisfied
been sitting here since ten
know nothing
3. a lost comb

and you don't feel dressed
do these clothes match
sometimes it seems
as if clothes are needed
to count the weeks
1. as dinner progresses
the conviction grows
even calmed down
of course there's no must
but it goes so smoothly

I miss the water
2. a funny discovery
my atlas is right
she's standing by the river
and stares into the distance

the banks touch each other
she's not yet there
3. needs a moment
she has to eat
reach the place
where the river stops
1. small fork
probably in the riverbed
for my part
they'll stay for a day

sell their stuff
leave the country
2. vice versa
what she finds for food
she will get through

on the walk to the place
where the river stops
crosses borders
3. constant organising
1. you can't drink
from which glass
you know sometimes
at night when I close my eyes
I hope the disaster
will have become less big

2. definitely use
and you can talk
you can read what it says
the duckling rolls out of the handkerchief
once on the same table

the little bird collapses
suddenly disappears into thin air
some tiptoe around the box
3. you're attracting attention
maybe we'll be friends
who's happy about that
living on the mainland
sleeping in a bed at night
when there's an island nearby
1. getting used to the thought or

actually that's all I do
pitch a tent
not underneath the trees their foliage
but next to it
on fixed days

that can be found
by others
2. a run-up curve
like yesterday
between the fork of two
two heavy branches
still quietly
keep repeating
3. except for
when there's no wind

they won't come
there'll be nothing for us to do
risky to go boating sailing
no wind no fight
1. light arrest

2. next to the hands forehead
in a triangle on the ground
we talk before the start
about what we think
about the rain
which is refusing to come down
3. while it didn't cross
anyone's mind
to get rid of the branches
when you're alone

you have more time
to do stuff
go down to the boat
1. just in case
you're right

it might be better
to go to sea
together
stay together
drop a bottle in a bucket
then you know for certain
it's us
not the enemy
2. tacking through the sand
against the wind

do you think I've got a funny walk
this whole time
I've been wearing wellies
to get to the water
3. wait

I fill the glass
the difficulty is
I can't
climb to the top
carrying the entire box
in my hands
1. nobody's satisfied
been sitting here since ten
know nothing
because of the strong wind

more than half
of the bread
ends up in the water
2. what am I wearing
my trousers are covered in sand

a grey cloud shifts
into the blue net
do you always land softly in green
3. deep breaths
bent arms
drinking wild water
how wonderful
would it be
to wind up
in this cloud

with one jump
caress each other scratch
stroke
1. the familiar is back
next to the forehead hands

in a triangle on the ground
this will be a memory
small fires burn everywhere
for cooking on
2. get nothing out of this
like yesterday
looking being bored
being restless
the feet a little apart
without a book on the head

listening to make sure
here another glass
3. I saw the sea first
fill the box with books
pass round again

so much really to see
the tree
just above that branch
in the middle
is the horizon
1. the ducks are back to front
when I reach the other side
without touching the ground
shouldn't someone cook
then why the rush

to be in a hurry
2. the map as straight as
possible in my hand
with a torch
in the other

breaking off pieces of chocolate
 you'll eat anything
you can find
on a seized ship
1. joyously nervous
lean back
with my ears
in the water like this
for the first time
the sun

can set more quickly
then again no
1. dark again
not too close
to the reeds

where the lilies grow
not too far from shore
the battle with the lilies takes time
another thing
2. no light anywhere
possibly the marines
express
their waiting differently
than the rest
who knows what they call to mind

3. shortly after each other
1. lower than the sea
a starling
on the branch of the elderberry
to wait

we had to stay
together
not wander off by ourselves
2. arms and legs
turned inwards
that's completely over
there they come
he has found her
never brings anything new
3. moreover

what I managed
to accomplish
I won't repeat
again
1. lines run across the field

once I leave
something must have changed
barely touch the food
return the scraps
to the kitchen
2. briefly then
like a short stay
briefly needs to be then briefly
or in a box
I like boxes

the first couple of days
we slept in a box
3. leaves
broken off trodden on
someone passed by here

didn't take the trouble
to hide his presence
1. of course we know
where they are
where the leaves
are processed
you can just go there
 watch the lorries
pull out
2. why wait

for change
change only
deep in thought
about a chair
to chew for a long time

3. wonderful
today's somebody's birthday
food on the boat
for a change
1. lilies again
like new
don't respond
every time
something comes up
the branch on the left right

on the left again
on the right the branch
and all done
2. what remains
is the most important

and the most important
you can see
what they're burying
and are planning
to return
3. quickly get up
the observer can wait
the fish can't
has to be eaten
warm

SWALLOWS GO

1. basket
make visible
you're in the park
you hide behind a tree
which we all have to
think about

2. of course I look
can catch them
then I quickly look away
no way for you to know
if you were gone
for long
3. follow by day
at some distance
split the supplies

in two
1. oh getting lost is
no longer an option
and it concerns
a considerable amount
for a repetition

no longer
to be an option
2. how many pheasants
the gamekeepers
release each year
nobody knows
nobody wants to go
if we have to go back
we'd rather go after all

3. just means
more work
has mister bos
put the vases back
in the ground
for this evening

1. ever onwards
2. many people
come carrying vases
they don't want to
put down
the ones they've chosen
aren't finished yet
3. actually in the water
they're just right

we continue talking
if they're not just right
you're free to go
it'd be terrible
to have to go home
for the journey home

half a journey
is the journey home
4. sighs wearily
every time he
serves out a deep plate
they protect each other
know things
to use
towards each other

5. closed
it must be spring
6. there's stripes at the door
like the sun on the ferns
let's forget
how often people talk

at cross-purposes
7. in the rain
I saw it yesterday
is it different
work hard
want to rehearse
quickly take over
8. why only
when another

can do it too
is another
cumbersome
be embraced
9. drinking in whispers
only the trade

is satisfied
I need to be in the park
by dusk
where we assemble
in a high elm
tomorrow we leave first thing
1. few clouds
the rest is done
think faster

than the rest
at the risk
of having so much strength
left over
2. wet shrubs
by morning

something else happens
she walks round
the back of the shrubs
then he wakes up
but doesn't follow
because he knows her well
3. drinking in whispers
you'll see
how happy you'll be

if you stay
in the mud
you are nowhere
the rain will see to that
1. look the sea
2. a conch

you can no longer leave
you look at me
what's on your mind
a dip
whoever stays in the longest
has to take care
of dinner
3. the same sunset
if I need a break

all good
1. all of a sudden
we're swimming
fast as we can
as if we're
lifelong friends

2. the same sunset
if I need a break
all good
3. the ducks are back to front
when I reach the other side
without touching the ground
shouldn't someone cook
then why this haste
to get a move on

4. better
sit and lean
against the mast
against who else
feed the ducks
no wind no fight

to take aim at
5. let's wave
wave back
I've been spotted
are planning
to moor in this spot
6. yellow flowers
the first tones sound
guilty what for

guilty of what
didn't do anything
he was already gone
before I got here
7. beauty on a string
in the water

don't know
what they play
at least a day
that I lost
to hear listening
they walked in
8. stays in the glass
until the glass is empty
you'll see

every day
she comes closer
don't try
to touch her
stand in her way
9. under the tree

that acts as a lighthouse
they seek shelter
from the sun
find food
regularity
1. as if on their own
her feet float to the surface
it has to be her
we know the currents

if you play here
you'll need insurance
know how to live
2. hello moon
so low in the sky
am in such pain

can't sleep
send everyone away
am I afraid
3. in the air
all is well
as soon as you swing
down again between the branches
the chain yanks itself into place
1. a heavy chain

lifts her up
it silences the crickets
so often when she dozes off
slide clatter clanging back into place
the moon has found her
2. black always looks good

were the first words that came
you'll never get the smell
out of your clothes
3. along with a large parcel
from the south
here she comes again
every day
you should know
what she eats

1. here she comes again
misunderstood by her surroundings
she throws her head back
2. gold paint smudges
3. put them in a box
and set to work

you'll get a lot in return
there's no point
sitting
on an island
4. hairs everywhere
there's no point
sitting
on an island
this is years ago

just a thought
on the other side of the ocean
5. put them in a box
and set to work
nothing can escape
6. the animals slide

off the sandbank
soundlessly enter the water
it's an equal fight
a lovely day
7. it's a lovely day
she's all scrunched up
for a visit
to the boomdijk
things have yet to settle down

the work is yet to be finished
8. when the afternoon train
rumbles across the river
she descends
for the sheer pleasure
of climbing alone

and to get to know
the tree better
9. the river has emptied
there must be
an explanation
somewhere
she's different from the cargo
doesn't come back leaves me
with the others

1. then as long
as I travel
I no longer hear that voice
as soon as I stand still
she returns and so does
that same clacking sound

that stroking of the hand
across my back
2. somebody touches me
gently pats my back
in the neck
strokes my nose
running means running
for a car
travelling

travelling for a car
3. she lights
a lantern
hoists it
fastens the rope
it gives off a quiet light

she thinks about
swimming
out there
far away from the island
seeing
what it looks like
from the water
1. a round patch
of ferns

flattened
someone lay there
an owl hoots
on the other side
it's the captain
she hoots back

2. the captain leans forward
touches the grass
with his hand
it isn't warm
it can't stay warm
for long
3. carefully stick
my head sticks
out over the roof

of the car
for quite some time
I remain immobile
before someone
notices me
1. awkwardly slow

so that all or nothing passes
a silence falls
that isn't to say
why are you heading
that way
she's fallen asleep
2. on an island
together
to know

what we know
on arrival
they are left undisturbed
but what happens
when they return
3. the forest won't die

it changes
when you tell them
nobody wants to go
if they have to
they'd rather after all
4. damaged by itself
it's yellow
and invisible
if every gesture

produces a sound
then every gesture
is preceded by a sound
5. how can I
see the island
as you see it

and just for what it is
I sleep late
then I don't sleep
6. only strangers
don't make detours
on the mainland
people react differently
when a guest frequents more often
he wants to be recognised

7. hello moon
so low in the sky
am in such pain
can't sleep
send everyone away
if I'm afraid

8. get changed in silence
everything is old
there can't be
much work
9. a brown label
hangs from every object
are on their way
focused on work
don't talk much to each other

1. hello moon
so low in the sky
am in such pain
can't sleep
send everyone away
if I'm afraid

2. the berries ferment
singing alone
is harder
than the memory expectation
we cherish
the branch itself
is beautiful
to sling
a rope over

3. hello moon
so low in the sky
am in such pain
can't sleep
send everyone away
am I afraid

1. barking in the dunes
you can blow
all you like
sometimes it's cardboard
the light falls on the vases
on the cardboard
sometimes it's far away
in the absence of wind
how important

is the light
very important
you see my hand
her hand goes up
I see your hand
keep it there

before dark
2. black duck
miraculous stain
can be moving
when not one part
of the everyday
has been included
however minuscule this part
it's inviolable

3. look the sea
1. must endure pain
only talks
about what I know
about the submarines
again

the submarines haven't been
sold
3. red flower
jump
back and forth
with water
in that way
I never know
where I am

3. keeps colliding
we're faced with the decision
to dispatch not dispatch
we could
build
a submarine

4. four traffic cones
5. a half-submerged hide
the bridge across the river
is heavily damaged
a nearby refinery
apparently
caught fire
6. if so the work
has been for nothing

the large floodlight
is the swallow
but which boat
is the smaller one
7. until beyond
the half-submerged hide

dark grey is softer
darker blue
I'm not saying
you have to swim
quite the opposite
be embraced
8. wet shrubs
of course
hurry up

or you'll miss them sailing by
you have to choose
between the chain and your life
or give me the chain
and I'll take you
to the other side

9. the nuts fall
from the trees
break apart
he lifts her up
and feels her tightening muscles
in his arms

ARM SIGNAL

2. arm signal
3. a monkey acted out all quarrelsome
and bit in the captain's thumb
the captain flew into a rage
and locked the monkey in a pretty cage
4. the moon
slowly climbs higher

in her cold light
wild dogs glide by
stand still and catch a whiff
of the lonely monkey
1. this is a boat
no way I can
wait for you

all day
2. make a loop
in the air
must be a bridge
to be sure
they shout a bridge
3. who said

I'm not attracted
to stripes
if I have space
I'll paint that white as well
1. at ease
where's the bridge
when it's been raised

2. a woman sits
in the restaurant
a woman with a small dog
eats white meat
3. slows down
finally pulls up
beside her

1. light but slow
when summer comes
they move
up the slope
I don't think of this as standstill
2. you suspect
something iron

something's off
when you get upstairs
all you are is tired
a little later on pride wells up
3. it's summer
there's not a lot of folk
the distance flows

like a calm sea
the ripples of memory
1. for a fish
those areas don't exist
and following animals
through the generations
isn't easy

he has to try
and determine
the genetic adjustment
from the incongruous
2. you won't see
anything in me
having come up

if I don't come down
on the other side
anything that's not from the west
we call eastern
1. heavens
you're cold
builds up a supply

not through production
complaining is part of life
2. round ears
3. round nose
then I side by side
we gallop into the water
recognition drift

made good by the wind
when he returns the monkey
and I know it's at home
its spirits will revive
1. places a hand on
his arm
but it's as if floating

her fingers
above that arm
2. in the wind
sour colour
makes the rounds
a herd
approaches

1. who they belong to
she dances backwards unaware
perhaps silence is also
a comparison
and dreams
one hour a day
before I buckle down

to work
2. quickly put back
it's possible in threes
everyone knows
what he or she gets
so no one
will be disappointed

1. for the birds
2. for the birds
3. the faster you build
the shorter
it will stand
the sooner there's work
4. will only help

if there's water
their work makes the ground
increasingly valuable
5. digging in the same location
makes the ground
increasingly valuable
6. for the birds

1. calm
on those vases
a different treatment
of the sea
equally is evidence
of a different providence
1. from a broken object

there's something telling
about a broken object
whether she turns on the light
go for a walk
sits in a boat
3. this way
he'll never get used to me

oh points back
and is too long
closed for too long
a moonless night
to be precise
there's so much talk
1. nothing forces

the half-moon sinks
behind the grey cloud banks
over the mountain tops
spreading west
2. a bird flies
through the air
straightaway my dog

sits on its tail
1. travelling is something
you have to learn
slows down
to let the road
last longer
2. what did he do

she runs off
he follows her
through the tall summer grass
higher and higher
they go
slowly bend away
towards the south

1. the acoustics sheer pleasure
2. the meadows begin
3. somebody chops with an axe
in a piece of wood
that makes a sound
4. they continue chopping
but now just

for the sound of it
5. I'm sure
when it's supported
by certain sounds
and a flowing rhythm
the work will turn out better
6. turns up every day

to work
it's my boat
1. forces me
to keep working
which suits me fine
long ago I learned
to work

surrounded by lots of people
2. it annoys me
that he has more courage
than I side by side
we gallop into the water
3. sometimes she talks
about herself

in beautiful english
tries to explain
how she can't see
the island around her
but has the distinct feeling
the deer are watching her
1. she gets up

the deer do too
and so we stroll
through the damp forest
2. look the sea
one feels more
important than the other
and everyone listens

to what
the other says
1. that's why he isn't laughing
in his eyes
only boredom
will not abandon him
2. dries off his arms

a starling lands
outside the lines
on the green stretch of grass
and it's my fault it hops across
onto the battlefield
3. and another
boredom feeling

is boredom feeling
without a detour
every note plops
in its rightful place
1. from drivers'
grievances
why not

side by side
can you see anything about me
2. the work
carries on a while
in silence
3. does grief recoil like a spring
I lay them side by side

without humans
the landscape
would be less varied
1. arm signal
2. as soon as a dog gets a whiff
it stands still
I don't think of this as standstill

cheers me up
3. somebody stands
to one side
to take over
the work
4. through whatever accident
if I don't stop now

I'll never stop
and not just
because I want to know
what happens next
1. just look
what you are lying on
goudriaan

is it conceivable
soft mumbling
2. I can't understand
where they went
or can I use them
loses its equilibrium
3. falls flat on the ground

no it isn't like that
just look
what you're lying on
1. through my fault
someone standing
on the sidelines
will take over

the work
2. quickly replace
it's possible in threes
everyone knows
what he or she gets
so no one
will be disappointed

1. what remains
is more important
and what is more important
can you see
what they are burying
and intend to
to return

2. the sea has warmed up
I ask myself
where he's gone
the leaves fall
the first skim across the lawn
keen to hold on
to their head start

1. trembling left hand
a ladder
woven together from twigs
is a more beautiful symbol
for that vague longing
2. in me
I notice that

many people
feel that too
follows
3. to encircle
her absence
along the coast
the contours of the peninsula

1. when the leaves have fallen
the moon returns
over the lake
2. round so it seems
as if intentionally
dug up
3. now and then

his paws
twinge
as if he's still walking
4. light but slow
like a pink ball
here or there
look at the animal

she can't see it
but as a dark object
that keeps getting bigger
1. it's as if death
has made the monkey
one with the tree
or a piece of petrified fruit

that slowly grows from it
reaches the ground ripened
to witheringly
surrender its seeds
2. gives him a hand
and lies down beside him
if she could measure

her length
with his
1. give him a hand
and lie down beside him
if you can measure
your length
with his

BIG BATTEN

1. hands up
2. young shoots
bend light
their outstretched necks
immobile then
3. circled entirely
by water
as if someone
committed a crime
4. partly I do it
finish it
it's done
and forgotten
1. one

finds himself
on a ship
out of the harbour
thinking further
he finds himself
at sea
2. two
they have a car
when will they leave
just after sunset
3. if I do it
I feel small
because he takes large steps
how he does that
gets it together
another meaning

4. in the forest four lean
against the car
speak in whispers
to each other
while staring at the
shore
1. there's someone down there
2. I ask him
will you stay down
there
2. I ask him
do you want us
to stay
3. three in the car
returns
with hands full of wood

he looks about satisfied
I found that wood
4. I ask him
will you stay
down there
1. the sun breaks through
which doesn't mean
the light
that can't pass through
the object
is held back
2. walking around it
doesn't yield
any additional information
3. the shadows
of the trees

slip and shift
with the sun
to the west
first rise
4. try walking
around a basket
while your face
remains focused
remain focused
on the wicker basket
1. more
a hound
round
it seems
as if deliberately
dug up

2. under the weight
of the ripening nuts
as the shadows grow
longer
in the evening dusk
3. for another
the portent of
an approaching ship
4. the portent of
an approaching ship
keeping your hands
together
like so
unpleasant in fact is
a menacing question
1. the shadows

of the trees
slip and shift
with the sun
to the west
2. by not thinking
the same over and over
the boat has
become incredibly bigger
when nothing is done
the collection risks
falling apart
this summer
3. forty seven
4. almost dead straight
from the ground up
because standstill

begins exactly at
the most risky point
when greatness
lies within reach
1. I should stop
because standstill
begins
at the most risky point
2. smiles too
takes my hand
tucks something in
white lace
fine weather
3. the sun
in the far west
the entire boat

the events
succeed one another
there where they occur
the shadows stand
4. take possession
of the trees
of the desire
of the monkey
only to return
1. the same shore
I ask him
which doesn't mean
a boat drifts away
when somebody
finds the empty boat
thinks that

I have drowned
2. I you we
in spring
I grow quieter
the leaves appear
on the trees
I can no longer see her
3. and so in the storm
the leaves fall
from the trees
into the water
4. another
and another
1. splits

PILOTAGE I

1. a moment alone
comes into leaf
flower discolour
shed leaves
2. recently deceased
3. for those who travel
further west
I'll stand here
twenty minutes long
4. and thus it storms
the leaves fall
from the trees
into the water
and I come back to life
1. I you we in spring
I grow quieter

the leaves appear
on the trees
I can no longer see her
2. for me certainly
a pilot
keeps irregular hours
dan: eternal grin
3. replace only
with immediately
when later
on the boulevard
you meet amorata
tell her hi from me
and tell her that
pilot zwart
has gone back to sea

4. molten lead
like a grey heron
still there's
not only
this silence that lack of incident
that's responsible for
1. the water level
dark and still
will last
as long as I want
this year
summer has come
early
2. just like that
against the pain
what does someone do

who's the only one to see
besides is happiness
perishable
3. this summer
I'm trying
to pretend
I'm a visitor
dan: eternal grin
4. only a large ripple
on the water
where he went under
1. the photographers
push one another aside
the water is cold and
sea
2. the harbour

filled in
if the emotions are never visibly
smoothed over
3. the smaller boats
are moored to the pilot boat
side by side
just stay calm
I'll lift you
into the boat
and you too
4. the smaller boats
are moored
to the pilot boat
side by side
because if I don't
she'll worry so

she'll think
he's gone
1. meanwhile
wrap him
in a blanket
lucky thing
I had to be
on board
2. where's the wood
how can that be
should I ask him
to close his eyes
to get a better look
you should ask him
to shut his eyes
3. a running man

4. for a pilot
even with a pilot
on board
the captain stays
in charge of the ship
dan: captivated
1. keeps dragging
all sorts to the bottom
which you think is beautiful
it's still quiet down there
2. on the bottom
3. there are constants
everyone's looking for something
recognisable
a thought
can take on a solid shape

as if drumming up
the past
will attract tourists
drawing it closer to
something of an
explanation
4. lasts now
for as long as I want
further west
sailing becomes travelling
and is considered
more and more important
1. further west
sailing becomes travelling
and more and more important
2. all sorts

which you think is beautiful
now it's still quiet there
perhaps she's dancing
perhaps he let her
go
3. what I learn
there are words
about which you can
discover absolutely nothing
I guess
a few hundred
4. you're not up
to anything
but stand for something
empty dancer
knows the moves

but collapses on the sand
1. it's about something
you can't articulate
the beauty of dance
2. apartment to let
3. until summer
so beach combing
will soon be over
no I'll start
a new collection
do you want to start
a collection for someone
I'm lucky enough
to build
a collection
for someone

4. what's escaped me
1. slow down
what does someone do
who alone saw
something
2. it's summer
not a lot of folk
about
3. sometimes we
look each other up
so as not to become
completely alone
4. in the distance
lies the other pilot boat
lies waiting
until a ship

needs her
1. the running man
2. if you think
it's time
to take a rest
3. tick tick
what about him
attracts you
he wants to know
how strong I am
4. back in a tick
what about you
attracts him
he wants to know
how strong I am
1. if you think

it's time
to take a rest
the longer I'm with you
the more dependent
I will be
2. should I ask him
to shut his eyes
the longer
I'm with you
the less dependent
I will be
3. quo vadis
tramp trade
4. whereto
looks yellow
on the horizon

probably better
it's nothing
1. sailors
savour things
sweet
2. questions
to which I knew the answer
I left to one side
started with a question
I had to think
about
for a long time
3. he keeps returning
to the same place
from which he left
again

4. would be a pity
I'm still
savouring
last night's
sun-swept wind of spring
1. spreads his arms
do I expect
the monkey
will leap into them
2. to the wave
3. on the edge
of the bridge
she feels at home
she watches
the daft dance
of a young wave

you'll catch your death
4. wait till tomorrow
the wood belongs here
the soft sounds
the monkeys taught me
an orange vase
deep glass dishes
just keep serving them out
1. lucky thing
I had to be on board
sun-swept wind of spring
2. the first one asked
in a dark coat
too big for me
what does it matter
3. the ship

the ship ran its course
out of sight
I have to believe them
don't change
they become extinct
4. on the quay
1. on the quay
I was sitting on the quay
watching
and so was she
2. black belongs
in 3.
in the water
3. with a duck
4. when
he returns

to the same place
from which he left
again
1. at the bedding
the water beats up foam
whilst water
runs off them
the far bank
turns
into mud
2. from north to south
inseparable little ducks
bob up and down
beak to beak
tail to tail
the rest invisible

3. running man
no one wonders
how I manage
any of this
4. travelling is something
you can learn
slow down
to let the road
go on for longer
1. to the summer
will it influence growing old
to the leaves
falling from the trees
in the park
to an evening
like yesterday's

2. while we
think about each other
3. barks
at the waves
a milky haze
in one eye
in that one he's blind
4. moreover
turning to the sun
how to divide
the available attention
bearing in mind
the tourists
who in summer
couldn't care less
about change

MUDDLED MOLENWATER

then the arms
the white hair
blown
by the wind
across his face
2. full of
paint
stains
water
1. walk
around the car
but wherever
I look
only trees cars
2. valuables at the bottom

it's as if
they sway
you came after all
where's the rest
gone far-flung

1. same again please
the battle
with the trees
goes on
for hours
2. taunt
those monkeys
on the opposite bank

1. under the car
slightly bigger
2. than the moon
1. under the car
slightly bigger
than the moon
2. half
of all accidents
happen
in the dark
from behind
home
before dark
1. rough bang
2. nut in one hand
1. hand

grabs neck
neck nods head
head touches leg
leg twists hip
hip twists torso
and that to the power of four

2. in a black bucket
filled with water
stares it down
2. clean up the mess
caused by
the increasingly weakening sun
late september
1. and early october
inspects me from head
to toe
2. spreads
his arms
just for a moment
1. get the signal
stretch both arms wide

spread both legs
and let him get on with it
let him pat me down the clothes
2. hands
1. what they seek
2. a collision
is thankfully averted
beautiful tail

look it's over there
1. for hours
the battle
with the monkeys goes on
2. taunt those trees
on the opposite bank
slowly through
their colour supply

CHESTNUT JOE

a cheerful evening

1. swaying
ashen backs
of elephants
like grass in their lilting past
shake the bushes
tear off a few branches
to chew on pensively

2. the cook
for the food

3. for a westerner
what westerner
does not have

a cheerful evening
his cheerful evenings

1. chestnut joe

2. at the piano
the whole day

3. rolls back
it's the cold
of the night before
the cold has got a hold
on us

1. rolls back
it's the cold

of the night before
the cold has got a hold
on us

2. at the piano
the whole day

3. chestnut joe

1. I cheerfully
begin again
what do we see
when our eye
is not constantly
eclipsed
by recoiling eyelid

2. the cook
for the food
beams broadly
3. has lost
meaning since
a permanent river crossing
is being built
on the horizon
1. at the end
of the day
when everyone wants to go home
at once
2. during the construction
of that new bridge
during gale-force winds
a serious accident

a blockade
of that bridge
3. to the others
who with grand gestures
draw through the air
how the bridge should be
1. this time I walk into
the park
from the back
even as the treetops
touch each other all over
2. I look
at the other walkers
only earth nameplates
on stems
of bare plants

it pleases me
to look
as if there are nuts
3. not only
the surroundings disappear
the object too
on which initially
the attention was focused
1. she's absolutely right
what you've seen
too often no longer works
this is how monkeys play
2. a double role
3. until we've had enough
1. by evening helicopter
they are shattered

when finally
together

1. the newspaper drifts

2. across the room
the rest is silence

3. it's good
that seldom
leaves
the living room
of the owner

1. it's good
that seldom

HACK TONES

1. first come
one two three
whereto
you'll see
2. you don't say that
at the mill
3. that's what you say
on the dyke

1. shoot back and forth
under the leaves
the tiny dances
which are there
from the start

2. the evening starts
downstairs
3. all the shadows teem with roses

1. all the shadows teem with roses
2. long lines
and every track
its own shadow
3. slowly apply
roses changes

are unstoppable
1. stroke
with a little luck
I'll break even
2. sit
3. sit
1. can divert attention

attention will come
almost completely
by pushing
on his strong point

2. sit
3. irritating repetition
what is too much
the sun sinks
under the leaves

HACK TONES

touch
1. on the pond
the left follows
the clock's hands
2. on the pond
while no one
has thought of
removing those branches
3. bent out of shape
more resigned
to stumbling
in the dusk dark
to brooding
and remembering
than to deliberate
a strategy

4. baskets
barrels
fretting
1. in the winter months
it's
2. a revealing exercise
probing
the progress of poverty
in our country
3. orange

4. and in what way
or rather
in what form
people protect themselves
against this
1. one means loss
because adjustment is required
which doesn't mean
you can't talk
about something
that isn't finished yet
2. with peel and all

3. kraa kraa kraa

4. oh waddles
around satisfied
when it's
stroked
with friendly grunts
4. but his stature
serves to determine
the size
of things
4. back to small

know that many
climb into their cars
after work
to earn some extra cash
as chauffeur
1. right foot
counterclockwise

2. in the way
nature will
on the other hand
order is
more and more bound
to the appearance
3. the mimicking
of sounds
of certain birds
like owls ravens
rasp
4. again I walk into
the park
from the back
while the treetops
all over each other

OUTER BUOY

darker than now
for fear
for his safety

4. add up
the numbers
in every possible way
the same answer

3. when the door
of the watch house
for the ferry
opens

the sea comes
blowing in
2. the cook in the kitchen
sings along

1. before dinner
I will reach the sea
2. before dinner
I will reach the sea

3. kitchen
kitted out like an airport
on which newspapers
are spread out

always between
the same banks
4. concentration of birds
3. sing lustily

only to duck and disappear
to an unknown destination
the crowds for the weather
unclear instructions a miscalculation

2. the sight of
the violently heaving
smoking boat
dulls drowning my appetite

1. steadier
across the waves
onto the next boat
without ever

dwelling a little longer
on whichever side
that may be
2. does shelter

make knowhow available
off to work
arms crossed
above the head

at the altitude of
a cloudless sky
3. hence the search for
a lot of time

and all at once
play footie together
4. before dinner
I will reach the sea

MILL IN THE SUN

a stationary walker
the first beginning
of such a swarm

a shrub
a dark stain on the ground
a stationary walker

yellow powder

1. low horizon

stick
quickly found
straight and generally round

how far
the particles
are apart

strokes
his hand
through the white hair

ALL AT SEA

what goes well

with what
1. pull loose

transformation of
minuscule air bubbles

a dab for starters

2. you're back
I said delighted
3. at the beginning

of the largest pier
in the world
4. you'd better ask
when you get upstairs
everyone laughs of course

a dab for starters

1. at the beginning
of the largest pier
in the world
2. you're back
I said delighted
things names
come back
all sorts all sorts

3. that that
is possible
of equal value
calms things down
red is urban sprawl

4. again
closer to each other
than before
carefully measure
with string again

1. again
closer to each other
than before
carefully measure
with string again

2. phew becomes
calmer
beauty
on a piece of string
3. on the waves

a boat

4. becomes
calmer
if another one
is needed
1. sea keeps young

2. people at sea
signal
3. forever yours

4. across each other
1. en route
to the warm seas

2. usually ends
with the purchase
of a red vase

cheerful by nature

3. zinc
corrugated sheet

copper
over there it's
six hours earlier
than here

4. much too low
whole mosquito swarms
in their turn
mosquitoes attract birds
moving on

1. from
the difference
in starting times
and what about me
the material is
colder than before
2. by thinking

the same over and over
the boat
has become incredibly bigger
3. by four
4. by four
I really should
ask dawn

I emerge

1. sings of the sun
running upstairs

whatever happens
to that one particle
will show up
in the other
at the same time

2. pull loose
transformation of
minuscule air bubbles
3. weighs four kilos

I can walk around
with it for hours
4. or in a box
the past
sits in boxes
always alone

what I know
1. that an observed particle
gives an unpredictable shove 2.
3. away with it

4. in the spring
1. in the summer
much damage
to nestling birds
budding green
is pleasing
audibly relieved
2. I'm distracted

3. sailors
never think
about what they leave behind
4. what comes after

1. that and the fact
of staying on one's feet
up here

2. tidy up and count
stand dreaming
now 4.
3. beaks filled with mud

TWO PEEPS

the what
the what
the what
the what
the what
the what
the what
the what
the what
the what
the what
the what
the what
the what
the what
the what

hat

lies
one day
3. down
part of a house

that everything
is set
in motion

both
mean
the same bird

that everything
is set
in motion

invalidate
measurements
his measurements
my measurements
1. gulp
it's your turn

the road
to the forest
that's no longer
being used

2. that's one
the road
to the forest
that's no longer
being used

3\. exciting
finally
an examination

that's one
the stalk
stays attached
to the stone

the stalk
stays attached
to the stone

1. of the aforementioned
2. or did the addressee
mean
the sense
of having come up
with the idea by himself
exciting

to go through
an examination
for a change
3. someone's coming

on one side
the branches
of the trees
start lower down
than usual
note a 1.

2. skin hair eyes
3. smile
a signal
you have nothing to fear
go on choose
and then you choose
of course
all sixteen

1. in the afternoon

2. a rushed nurse

3. brings the food

however careful
the risk on the other hand

binoculars

1. in moonlight
2. surplus superfluous
3. a long season

1. saplings long season
2. the daily operation
3. a boat

followed
by the sun
and I no longer think
1. now I'm here

the fluff drifts
on the air
from the willows
poplar

days
that
fine weather

meadow flowers
on every table
2. gives a push 3.

3. the summer
in their paws
that wood
that everyone has

do they whistle

a variation

1. if you'll return
2. if by necessity
1. if you'll return

2. if by necessity
1. if you'll return
2. if by necessity

THE SUN IN THE PAN

turn
one after
the other
turn

turn
one after
the other
turn

even better

turn
one after
the other
turn

turn
one after
the other
turn

even better

turn
one after
the other
turn

turn
one after
the other
turn

4. even better

turn
one after
the other
turn

turn
one after
the other
turn

and again after the

turn
one after
the other
turn

turn
one after
the other
turn

or the other

turn
one after
the other
turn

turn
one after
the other
turn

3.

turn
one after
the other
turn

turn
one after
the other
turn

because it's that kind of an evening

turn
one after
the other
turn

turn
one after
the other
turn

4. THE SUN IN THE PAN

think before summer

turn
one after
the other
turn

turn
one after
the other
turn

here you go

turn
one after
the other
turn

turn
one after
the other
turn

here you go

turn
one after
the other
turn

turn
one after
the other
turn

here you go

(turn
one after
the other
turn

turn
one after
the other
turn)

2. and

turn
one after
the other
turn

turn
one after
the other
turn

and again after the
4. what changes
4. when nothing changes

did you mean
what changes
when nothing changes

or the other

(turn
one after
the other
turn

turn
one after
the other
turn)

DROP KICK

thing.'

thing.'

guess.'

thing.'

thing.'
    thing.'
everything.'

329

justified.'

per cent.'
with the sun.'
like with everything.'
away.'

333

yourself at home.'

matter.'
and gone.'
be gone.'
to work hard.'
see parallels.'

usually come back.'
hardening clay.'
already been sown.'
care about.'

miss.'

missed.'
also the reality.'

catch.'

makes a lot.'
custom.'
here.'

times.'

think the latter.'

b.'

too too.'
living proof.'
keep off.'
at the same weight.'
fortune.'

times.'

without corrections.'
so corrections then.'
round up.'

you hear the difference.'
thing.'
nothing small.'
oodles.'

possible maybe.'
lasting factor.'
tribute.'

of leaves.'
forest ground.'

unnoticed.'

per cent.'

per cent.'

Acknowledgments

With warm thanks to the Dutch Literary Foundation for its financial support for this book. Also to Hawthornden Castle in Scotland, Übersetzerhaus Looren in Wernetshausen, near Zürich, and the Vertalershuis Antwerpen for their generosity and hospitality in providing me with the things I needed to work on these translations. Thanks to Francis Jones and Judith Wilkinson for their insightful editorial comments on these translations at different stages of their development, and to Anne-Mariken Raukema for sharing her firsthand knowledge of the poems with me. Special thanks to publisher Aaron Kent for bringing this unique voice to an English readership for the first time. Last but not least, thank you to Dix, for the patience and trust he placed in this translator.

LEG JE ONRUST UIT